Speak Fluent Body Language

Unlocking the Secrets of Nonverbal Messages

Table of Contents

Chapter 1. Introduction

Step into an exciting world beyond words with our Special Report, "Speak Fluent Body Language: Unlocking the Secrets of Nonverbal Messages". This amazing journey is not about convoluted jargon or complicated theories, but a colorful exploration into the art of acting without speaking. We offer you a ticket to delve deep into the universe of subtle gestures, intriguing facial expressions, and eloquent postures that silently convey messages more powerful than spoken language. Enliven your communication abilities, enhance your interpersonal skills, and bring a spark of fascination to mundane interactions by unlocking the secrets of nonverbal cues. Come, join us as we navigate this interesting landscape together and transform your wordless interactions into a symphony of meaningful exchanges! This empowering knowledge is just a purchase away—get your copy of the report today!

Chapter 2. Understanding the Importance of Nonverbal Messages

From the dawn of time, humans have relied on a range of communication methods, including a language that transcends the boundaries of spoken word—nonverbal messages. These silent cues are universal in their essence and are tethered to our emotions and thoughts, lending a depth to our verbal communications, adding a layer of trust and authenticity that words often can't achieve. Nonverbal communication, or body language, is a versatile and powerful expressive tool, integral for conveying attitudes and feelings, and creating mutual understanding with others.

2.1. Elements of Nonverbal Communication

There are several distinguished elements of nonverbal communication that coalesce to convey messages without the spoken word. Understanding these elements can refine your ability to manipulate your own body language and discern others' nonverbal cues.

2.1.1. Facial Expressions

Facial expressions are significant contributors to nonverbal communication. They are often immediate, instinctual, and universal. The human face can remarkably express countless emotions without saying a word. Moreover, people of different cultures have similar facial expressions for basic emotions like happiness, fear, anger, surprise, sadness, and disgust.

2.1.2. Body Movement

The way people sit, stand, and walk can all convey nonverbal messaging. These movements, known as postures, often suggest a person's current state of mind. A hunched posture might suggest low spirits, while someone standing tall may demonstrate confidence.

2.1.3. Gestures

Gestures vary greatly across cultures – yet another complex nonverbal communication system. Pointing, waving, and using the hands to indicate numerical amounts are examples of such cues, each carrying its independent connotation.

2.1.4. Eye Contact

The eyes are, as they say, the windows to the soul. Maintaining eye contact indicates interest and engagement, while evading eye contact often translates into avoidance or falsehood.

2.1.5. Proximity

Each culture has unwritten rules about personal space. Encroaching on someone's personal space may signify aggression or intimacy, depending on the context.

2.1.6. Voice

The way something is said often carries more weight than what is said. A change in pitch, speaking rate, or volume can alter the meaning, often dramatically.

2.2. The Role of Nonverbal Messages in Communication

Understanding the importance of nonverbal communication cannot be overstated – it is said that nonverbal cues account for up to 93% of the total meaning of communication. This figure, however, may not apply to all situations, yet, it indicates that nonverbal communication is a critical aspect of human interaction.

2.2.1. Complementing Verbal Messages

Nonverbal cues add depth to verbal messages, offering hints about the speaker's true feelings and intentions. For instance, a person might say, "I'm fine," yet their nonverbal cues may reveal a different sentiment, like discomfort or disappointment. Thus, nonverbal messages offer a reality check, sometimes nullifying the verbally communicated message.

2.2.2. Replacing Verbal Messages

At times, nonverbal cues can even replace verbal messages. Simple gestures like nodding in agreement, shaking hands, or showing a thumbs-up have become accepted symbols of communication across cultures.

2.2.3. Regulating Interactions

Nonverbal communication acts as a traffic signal in a conversation. It directs when to pause, when to interject, and when it's time to change topics. Without these cues, conversations could be chaotic and interjections could be viewed as interruptions.

2.3. Nonverbal Communication and Relationships

One vital area where nonverbal communication holds considerable weight is in strengthening relationships. By perceiving the subtle nonverbal cues exhibited by people around us, we can develop a deeper understanding of their thoughts and emotions.

2.3.1. Connection Building

Long-lasting connections require empathy and understanding, which stem from correctly interpreting the nonverbal elements. Tuning into the subtleties can help solidify relationships, whether professional or personal.

2.3.2. Trust Building

Interpreting nonverbal cues often leads to increased trust and understanding. Accurately comprehending the messages conveyed through facial expressions, posture, or tone of voice fosters a sense of trust that strengthens bonds.

2.4. Misinterpretations in Nonverbal Communication

While nonverbal communication brings a wealth of benefits, it also presents the challenge of misinterpretation. Due to differences in cultural norms, personal biases, or unawareness, the messages sent may not match the messages received.

2.4.1. Cultural Differences

Appreciation of personal space, the meaning of certain gestures, use of eye contact – all vary across different cultures, and misunderstanding them can lead to unintended offense or confusion. Greater awareness of these factors can manage misinterpretations.

2.4.2. Personal Biases

Biases and prejudices can cloud interpretation. For instance, if you have a fixed opinion about a person, you may misread their nonverbal cues to fit your preconceived notions, distorting the message.

With a deeper understanding of nonverbal communication's importance, we are better equipped to navigate our interactions, fostering a more nuanced dialogue that goes beyond words. Utilizing this silent language effectively can lead to stronger connections, cohesive teamwork, and an overall enriched communicative experience.

Chapter 3. Cracking the Code: The Science of Body Language

Our quest starts in the realm of silent conversations, the science of body language. Humans, like other mammal species, carry forward an ages-old tradition of communicating through gestures, body postures, facial expressions – the elements that form our body language.

3.1. Science Behind Nonverbal Communication

Why is body language so important, one might ask? The answer is simple. While words can convey information, body language unveils feelings, attitudes, and underlying thoughts. According to psychologist Albert Mehrabian's pioneering research, if an individual's words conflict with their body language, the listener is likely to trust the nonverbal cues over the verbal ones.

In cognitive science, body language is deciphered through two primary types of nonverbal cues: spontaneous and symbolic. Spontaneous cues are involuntary and often reveal genuine emotion or response. They include physiological reactions, such as blushing or yawning. Symbolic cues are voluntary actions learned from our cultural environment, like waving goodbye or nodding in agreement.

3.2. Deciphering Body Posture and Movement

Body posture and movement, collectively referred to as 'kinesics', form the bulk of nonverbal communication. Researchers divide kinesics into five main categories: emblems, illustrators, affect displays, regulators, and adaptors.

- Emblems: Gestures that stand for specific verbal meanings, like a thumbs-up for 'good job'.

- Illustrators: Gestures complementary to speech, giving emphasis or enhancing spoken words.

- Affect displays: Expressions of emotion, such as smiling.

- Regulators: Nonverbal cues controlling conversation, like maintaining eye contact.

- Adaptors: Unconscious movements revealing inner state, scratching head when uncertain, for instance.

3.3. The Eyes Have It: Unlocking Ocular Nonverbal Cues

Eye contact is one of the most direct and powerful forms of nonverbal communication. It can indicate interest, attention, attraction, and dominance. Direct and prolonged eye contact often conveys interest and attraction, while averting one's gaze suggests submission or discomfort.

Pupil dilation is another key ocular nonverbal cue. It's an involuntary response often linked to emotional arousal, potentially indicating interest, surprise or fear.

3.4. Beyond Words: Facial Expressions

Following close on the heels of ocular cues are facial expressions, potent indicators of emotional states. Universally recognized expressions include happiness, sadness, anger, fear, surprise, and disgust. The Paul Ekman's Facial Action Coding System (FACS) is an intricate method developed to quantify these expressions by measuring the movement of facial muscles.

Comprehending microexpressions, facial expressions that occur within a fraction of a second, can be instrumental in discerning covert emotions. However, detecting them requires keen observation and practice.

3.5. The Silent Dialogue of Arms and Legs

Arms and legs convey messages of their own. Crossed arms maybe indicative of defensiveness, while a confident speaker often stands tall with legs slightly apart. The position of legs and feet during a conversation can reveal interest or desire to exit.

Understanding the message legs and arms convey through their position and movement can give insights into a person's comfort level and emotional state.

3.6. The Power of Personal Space and Touch

The need for personal space varies from culture to culture, and violation of this space can provoke discomfort. Proxemics, the study of human spatial requirements, aids in navigating this delicate balance.

Touch, or 'Haptics', is equally significant. The context, duration, intensity, frequency, and location of a touch can mold its meaning. From a comforting pat on the back to a firm handshake, touch carries a spectrum of messages.

3.7. The Nonverbal Orchestra: Piecing It All Together

Interpreting body language isn't about assigning rigid meanings to gestures or expressions. It's about contextually analyzing a symphony of nonverbal cues. A genuine smile isn't just about turned-up lips, but also sparkling eyes and animated facial muscles.

Remember - body language is a continuous dialogue where every microgesture contributes to the overall narrative. Attaining fluency in this language requires observation, sensitivity, and practice.

As you venture deeper into the enchanting world of nonverbal communication, you'll find yourself unraveling hidden dimensions in everyday encounters. Whether you're defusing tension, building rapport, or simply making conversation, mastery of body language can lend you an edge. Unleash the power of the unsaid, understand the unspoken, and immerse yourself in the extraordinary dialogue of body language.

Chapter 4. Faces Tell Tales: A Glimpse into Facial Expressions

In the sphere of nonverbal communication, facial expressions emerge as one of the most potent tools, capable of conveying an array of nuanced emotions and intentions. The face, often coined as the mirror of the mind, holds the capacity to broadcast sentiments that words sometimes fail to express. As we navigate through this exploration of facial expressions, you will encounter how intricate muscle movements can unveil a gamut of information.

4.1. Unraveling the Basics

Understanding facial expressions first requires acknowledging our face as a complex landscape, composed of 43 distinct muscles. Each muscle, through its movements and contractions, contributes to the formation of some thousand possible facial expressions. Equipped with this knowledge, let's embark on the journey of unraveling the universal facial expressions, initially identified by psychologist Paul Ekman: joy, sadness, surprise, fear, disgust, and anger.

Joy is commonly expressed through a genuine smile. A genuine smile, technically termed the Duchenne smile, involves both the muscles around our mouth pulling up the corners of the lips, and the muscles around our eyes creating 'crow's feet'. Contrarily, sadness typically involves drooping eyes, downturned corners of the mouth, and sometimes includes tears. When conveying surprise, our eyes widen, our mouth opens, and our eyebrows arch up. Fear often mirrors surprise, but with the additional element of tension visible on the face. Disgust showcases a wrinkled nose, raised upper lip, and narrowed eyes. Finally, anger emerges through narrowed brows, flared nostrils, and hardened gaze.

4.2. Fine-tuning Your Accuracy

Understanding these basic expressions sets the foundation for interpreting facial expressions. However, fine-tuning your accuracy requires observing incongruencies, more subtle indications, and the context in which these expressions occur. A smile does not always indicate happiness—it could mask anxiety, discomfort, or politeness. Analyzing recurring patterns and pairing facial expressions with body language and verbal communication can aid in deciphering these hidden layers.

4.3. Temporal Aspects

Another crucial concept in evaluating facial expressions is their timing. Genuine emotions tend to be displayed briefly, around 0.5 to 4 seconds. Anything longer might indicate a 'masked' emotion or a social facade. Moreover, the moment when an expression occurs can denote whether it's a real or constructed emotion. Genuine emotions change swiftly in response to the stimulus.

4.4. The Microexpression

An intriguing component of facial expressions, microexpressions, is fleeting expressions that flash on a person's face for a tiny fraction of a second and reveal their true emotions. Microexpressions occur instinctively, making them virtually impossible to control. Hence, they serve as reliable tools for determining genuine emotions.

4.5. The Cultural Perspective

While the six basic emotions stand universally acknowledged, cultural influences substantially impact how frequently and openly they are expressed. For instance, cultures that value community harmony may encourage suppression of negative expressions like anger or disgust.

4.6. The Power of Emotion Recognition

Mastering the art of deciphering facial expressions can yield beneficial outcomes on both personal and professional fronts. Be it the negotiation table, social gathering, or a therapeutic session, interpreting facial cues can provide valuable insights about others' emotional states, intentions, and honesty, helping improve interactions and relationships.

4.7. Deception Detection

Understanding facial expressions also assists in detecting deception. Involuntary facial twitches or inconsistent expressions can signal dishonesty—though, one must exercise caution as these may also represent nervousness or discomfort.

With the journey reaching its conclusion, remember that interpreting facial expressions is not about judging but understanding and empathizing with others' emotions. This comprehensive insight takes you one step closer to mastering nonverbal communication. With practice and keen observation, you can transform your regular interactions into more profound, meaningful exchanges. The power of being able to 'read faces' is immense, but with it comes the responsibility to use this understanding ethically and empathetically.

Chapter 5. Saying It Without Words: Interpreting Gestures

We are often oblivious to the silent conversations we're engaging in every day. These silent dialogues are encoded in myriad gestures that we exhibit, either consciously or unconsciously. Gestures form an integral part of nonverbal communication, and being aware of what they mean can help us understand people beyond their words.

5.1. The Basics of Gesture

Body language is a form of visual communication, and just like every other form of communication, it has its vocabulary and grammar. It is made up of several elements, of which gestures are prominent. To begin understanding gestures, it's important to know the primary categories they fall into.

Adaptors: These are usually unconscious and can reveal how a person feels, like nail-biting indicating nervousness.

By categorizing gestures, we can more efficiently interpret them in different contexts. This categorization lays a foundation for a systematic approach to analyzing body language.

5.2. Gesture Zones

Just as words have different meanings depending on the usage, gestures also have different interpretations based on where they occur. Broadly, body language can be divided into three zones.

Lower Zone: This area refers to the section below the hips. Though these gestures are less observable, they often convey subconscious clues about our feelings, thoughts, and intentions.

Understanding these zones can help discern the intended meaning of a gesture, considering the area of the body employed.

5.3. The Gesture-Cluster Concept

It's important to remember that one gesture does not make a message. Avoid jumping to conclusions based on isolated cues. Instead, look for clusters of gestures—similar cues that reinforce a single message. A gesture cluster could look like crossed arms along with an averted gaze, signaling discomfort or defensiveness. A person might voice agreement, but if they follow it up with a deep sigh or look away, it's best to consider the possibility of their real feelings being otherwise.

5.4. Recognizing Common Gestures

While every person's body language can slightly vary based on their individual habits or cultural background, certain gestures are generally universal. Here, we roll out a brief guide to some common body gestures.

Hand-to-Face Gestures: These could be indicative of careful pondering, stress, or deceit, depending on the context and the rest of the person's body language.

Interpreting gestures effectively often requires sensitivity to the communicator's unique characteristics and the contextual surroundings. Therefore, being fully present during the interaction is crucial.

5.5. Gestures and Deception

Detecting deception is one of the most valued skills of reading body language. While it's not foolproof, understanding gestures can provide some hints. People often unconsciously display deceptive cues when lying, like sudden changes in gesture patterns, covering the mouth, touching the face more often, or displaying nervous ticks. Remember to look for gesture clusters and avoid jumping to conclusions based on a single cue.

5.6. Cultural Consideration in Gesture Interpretation

Culture has a significant influence on gestures. A gesture might carry one meaning in one culture and a completely different implication in another. Therefore, cultural literacy is essential when interpreting nonverbal cues, especially in our increasingly globalized world.

By learning to 'read' body language, we can create more empathetic and effective interactions with those around us. The power of gestures lies in their universal applicability—they underscore the essence of human interaction at its most primal level. Recognizing this art form in our everyday lives profoundly enhances our understanding of others and yes, ourselves.

This deep dive into understanding gestures, their categorization, areas of emphasis, and their meanings sets the groundwork for deciphering more complex nonverbal messages. Like any other skill, proficiency comes with practice. The more conscious you become of these nonverbal cues, the more fluent you'll become in the language of gestures.

Chapter 6. Of Postures and Positions: Body Angles and their Meanings

The human body communicates emotions, attitudes, and intentions without a word being spoken. Body postures and positions are a vital part of this nonverbal dictionary. Understanding the lexicon of body angles can help in deciphering the unspoken messages that people convey daily.

6.1. Myriad Meanings of Body Angles: An Introduction

Body angles are a subtext of body orientation. They give crucial details about a person's feelings and thoughts. Even when one is consciously silent, the body angles and orientation can unconsciously express dominant emotions.

People often fail to realize the unconscious messages they send through their body postures. These can be cues of interest, openness, attraction, distancing, confrontation, and dominance, among others. By reading body angles, you can achieve a deeper understanding of people's non-verbal messages.

6.2. Open and Closed Body Positions

One of the simplest but most revealing aspects of body language is whether a person presents a closed or open body position. This can drastically influence the tone of an interaction and reveal crucial details about someone's emotional status and perceptions.

Open body positions - When a person adopts an open position, it usually indicates that they are comfortable, relaxed, and receptive. People often unconsciously adopt an open position when they feel safe, welcome, or interested. This posture typically includes upright stance, uncrossed limbs, and facing the speaker directly. It indicates a high level of engagement, suggesting positive emotional states like happiness, fascination, or curiosity.

Closed body positions - Contrary, a closed position typically expresses discomfort, unease, or a lack of interest. This can include crossed arms or legs, hunched shoulders, or partially turned away from the speaker. This type of body angle indicates defensive or self-protective behavior. It signals that the person may not be open to interaction or is feeling defensive or introspective.

6.3. The Perception of Dominance and Submission through Body Angles

Body language can express dominance and submission. The intricate dance of power played out through physical posturing is primal and instinctive. Broad and open expressions generally communicate dominance or assertiveness, while smaller, self-guarding actions often indicate submission or defensiveness.

Dominant body language - Frequently, dominant individuals will stand tall, clearly marking their physical territory. They tend to occupy more space, typically keep their head high and use strong, relaxed postures. This language projects confidence and authority, and others may instinctively respond with submissive behavior.

Submissive body language - Conversely, submissive individuals often adopt smaller postures. They may cross their arms and legs, shrink their body size, and avoid direct eye contact. This kind of body angle communicates a desire to avoid conflict, or a lack of confidence or power.

6.4. The Dance of Attraction: Body Angles in Interpersonal Relationships

Body language is crucial in indicating romantic or platonic interest. A keen observer can often perceive the nature of a relationship through body language alone. Unlike spoken words, body language communicates more honestly, revealing true intentions and emotions.

Attraction and Interest - An interested person's body is typically pointed towards the person of interest, making use of open postures. Mirroring or copying the other person's body language also shows interest. The feet, interestingly, are often the most honest part of the body, pointing straight towards the object of one's interest.

Disinterest and Detachment - In contrast, when someone is disinterested, their body angles away from the other person. They may give the 'cold shoulder', literally and metaphorically. These unconscious cues give away the person's lack of emotional interest or engagement.

Body language is an unspoken language that we all use without realizing. Recognizing and interpreting body angles, open and closed positions, body language for dominance or submission, and those indicating attraction or disinterest, can greatly enhance our understanding of others. Whether it's in the business world, in interpersonal relationships, or simply in daily life, understanding this silent language presents a powerful tool for effective communication. Tune into these subtle cues, and turn each interaction into a symphony of meaningful exchanges.

Chapter 7. Looking Closer: The Significance of Eye Contact

In the realm of nonverbal communication, eyes hold an incredible amount of power. They're often described as the window to the soul, and for good reason. The slightest change in a person's gaze can communicate a full spectrum of emotions, intentions, and information—sometimes more accurately than words ever could. Mastering the language of eye contact can be a formidable asset, enhancing not only our understanding of others but also how we present ourselves to our world.

7.1. The Science Behind Eye Contact

Eye contact is not solely a human phenomenon—it has its roots deep in our evolutionary history, and it is inherent in numerous species. Primates especially rely on eye contact to establish social hierarchies and signal intentions. In human beings, this primal tendency has evolved and diversified, bringing about a nuanced language of glances, blinks, and stares that we interact with every day.

A scientific study by the National Institute of Physiological Sciences in Japan involves the use of monkeys to understand the neurological basis behind eye contact. The study found that particular neurons, called "eye cells," are activated solely during eye contact. Additionally, these eye cells seem to be directly linked with emotional processing meaning that the act itself of making eye contact elicits an emotional response. This suggests that not only are our brains hard-wired for eye contact, but there also seems to be an inherent link between eye contact and emotion.

7.2. The Psychology of Eye Contact

Beyond the fundamental, biological processes that underscore eye contact, we should also consider its psychological aspect. A number of psychological studies have verified the profound impact eye contact has on perception and interpersonal connection.

When someone maintains eye contact with us during a conversation, we're more likely to perceive them as trustworthy, confident, and emotionally stable. Eye contact can validate feelings and emotions—seeing someone's eyes light up as they smile can trigger a shared sense of satisfaction, just as catching the sympathetic look in someone's eyes can elicit comfort during times of distress. These are the principles of empathetic-mirroring, a unique process that aids in creating different emotional states.

7.3. Patterns and Meanings of Eye Contact

Eye contact serves as a kind of punctuation in the language of nonverbal communication; it controls the rhythm of conversation and interaction. However, among the varied meanings we convey through eye contact exist numerous patterns that we might not frequently notice.

- **Maintained eye contact:** This is often perceived as a sign of interest and engagement in the conversation. It can demonstrate respect, attraction, or even challenge, depending upon the context. Prolonged, unblinking eye contact, however, might come across as intense or threatening.

- **Avoiding eye contact:** Avoiding someone's gaze can signify a wide range of emotions like nervousness, discomfort, or even disinterest. It could also indicate deception, but context always matters. For instance, an introverted individual might find too much eye contact overwhelming and prefer to look away.

- **Frequent blinking:** Rapid blinking can denote stress or discomfort. However, a blink can also serve as a momentary pause or an expression of surprise.

Such nuances give necessary depth to eye contact as a mode of non-verbal communication. The real understanding lies in discerning this nuanced language.

7.4. Eye Contact in Different Cultures

Cultural interpretation of eye contact is as varied as cultures themselves. In Western societies, maintaining eye contact signifies attentiveness and honesty. However, in several East Asian cultures, excessive eye contact can be deemed disrespectful or aggressive. Understanding these cultural variations is crucial for appropriating eye contact into effective communication.

7.5. Applications of Eye Contact

Enhanced understanding of eye contact finds applications in numerous fields. In public speaking and leadership, eye contact can be a powerful tool to inspire trust and credibility. In interviews and meetings, it can highlight engagement and confidence. And in intimate relationships, eye contact can serve as an unspoken language of love and trust.

7.6. Enhancing Eye Contact

While the aptitude for eye contact can be innate, it's largely a learned skill. Incorporating practices like mindful observation, self-awareness exercises, and understanding different contexts can help improve eye contact. Training to use it consciously and effortlessly can be significantly beneficial for personal growth and effective communication.

7.7. Conclusion: The Power of Eye Contact

Eye contact is a critical aspect of nonverbal communication, capable of transmitting emotional states, regulating interaction, and expressing intimacy, power, and meaning. By mastering the subtle language of eye contact, we open a new avenue for human connection—one that goes beyond words, transcends spoken language, and gets directly to the heart of interpersonal communication. Mastering eye contact not only means understanding others but also expressing ourselves in a more nuanced and authentic manner.

Chapter 8. Feeling the Vibe: The Language of Emotions

As we embark on an exploration of the language of emotions, it's crucial to remember that our non-verbal communication often relays our feelings more accurately than words. This chapter will dive into details about how various emotions can be conveyed and understood through body language.

8.1. Recognizing Happiness

Feelings of joy or happiness are usually the easiest to recognize in others. When someone is genuinely happy, their eyes light up, and this is often accompanied by smiling. This doesn't mean a fixed, static smile but a fluid, changing expression. Open body language, such as relaxed arms and hands and a forward leaning posture, can also indicate happiness. Laughter, of course, is a strong indicator of joy as well.

8.2. Unmasking Sadness

Signs of sadness are usually quite distinctive from other emotions. Downcast eyes, a downturned mouth, and collapsed body posture could all point towards sadness. Other possible indicators include slowly moving or still hands and feet, and minimal eye contact. Being able to spot these signals can help you empathize with others in distress and respond in a supportive and considerate manner.

8.3. Detecting Fear

Fear can be a tricky emotion to decipher, as it often manifests similarly to surprise. However, fear often comes with wider eyes and raised eyebrows, more exaggerated than a simple startled note. The body might be pulled back, or there may be instinctive gestures to cover the face or body as if to shield oneself. Being able to recognize fear can be an essential tool in understanding situations where individuals feel threatened and necessitate a swift and compassionate response.

8.4. Identifying Anger

Recognizing anger can prove vital in navigating conflict. Signs you should watch for include a fixed, intense eye contact, a clenched jaw or fists, and a rigid, sometimes looming, body posture. The smoothness of expressions and movements often disappears when a person is angry. Detecting this inflammatory emotion can offer cues for you to either attempt defusing the situation or removing yourself from a potentially harmful atmosphere.

8.5. Interpreting Surprise

The expression of surprise usually lasts only a moment before transitioning into another emotion such as happiness, fear, or confusion. It generally includes a gasping mouth, wide eyes, and usually, raised eyebrows. The actual physical stance might not change much, but there may be a temporary freezing or halting of movement.

8.6. Recognizing Disgust

Signs of disgust are generally apparent. There might be a grimace or a wrinkling of the face, especially the nose area. In more intense cases, one might observe a physical step back from whatever has triggered the disgust. Detecting disgust can aid in understanding situations where boundaries have potentially been crossed.

Understanding the nonverbal language of motions is a complex task but mastering it can yield deeper insights into our interactions with others. The cues discussed in this section are general examples and may not hold true for everyone, as cultural and personal differences can influence nonverbal expressions of emotions. The key is to observe carefully, be open-minded, and considerate of these diversities.

8.7. The Role of Microexpressions in Emotion Detection

Prepared with the foundational knowledge of recognizing different emotions, we can delve deeper into the subtle world of microexpressions. Microexpressions are quick, involuntary facial expressions that happen within a fraction of a second. Despite their brevity, they are sincere indicators of one's emotional state and can be invaluable in detecting someone's true feelings.

8.8. The Influence of Culture

Discover how cultural influences shape our non-verbal communication styles and learn to navigate these nuances successfully. Understand that not all body language is universal, and considering cultural contexts when interpreting signs is essential.

8.9. Emotion Regulation and Body Language

Explore how the alignment of body language and emotions aids in emotional regulation—an essential tool in constructing a hospitable and compassionate environment. Find ways to handle your own body language signals to successfully manage your emotions.

8.10. Indirect Channels of Communication

Unveil the ways non-facial body language communicates emotions. From understanding the subtlety of gestures to deciphering the variety of postures, learn how to interpret these often overlooked yet significant communicative avenues.

At the ending phase of this chapter, it becomes evident that comprehending the language of emotions goes beyond the general face value reading of body signals. It involves an understanding of microexpressions, cultural influences, emotion regulation strategies, and non-obvious forms of communication. Recognizing and navigating these layers can significantly enhance your interpersonal skills and enrich your daily interactions.

Chapter 9. Decoding Nonverbal Signals in Key Social Settings

Nonverbal signals are a consistent feature in every human interaction. From the formal calm of business meetings to the exuberant chaos of social gatherings, they influence the course of conversations in ways that spoken words often can't. Without much ado, let's plunge into unravelling the mystery of nonverbal signals in key social settings.

9.1. The Role of Nonverbal Signals in Business Gatherings

Most professionals believe that the key to a successful business meeting lies in the quality of presentations, the potency of ideas, and brilliant debating. While these are undoubtedly crucial, nonverbal signals – the unsaid words – can make an immense difference in carrying your point across the boardroom table.

Territoriality is a classic element of power dynamics in business settings. High-ranking personnel establish their turf by dominating space, be it through a larger desk, a wider arm swing, or powerful postures that take up space. As an observer, it's valuable to understand this spatial hierarchy to appropriately gauge the power distribution in a meeting.

Postures and gestures can reveal a range of emotions. A clenched fist or crossed arms often indicate anger or defensiveness, whereas hands-open and leaning-forward postures hint at an open and receptive mindset. Spotting these gestures can help you adapt your message delivery or negotiation strategies.

Eye contact, a crucial nonverbal signal, helps to establish connection and trust. A steady gaze conveys confidence and honesty. However, constant eye contact might be perceived as intrusive or dominating. Hence, maintaining a fine balance is the key.

9.2. The Significance of Nonverbal Cues in Social Gatherings

Social gatherings, albeit more rogue and unstructured than professional meetings, have their unique dynamics that can be comprehended using the language of nonverbal signals.

Personal space, or proxemics, is especially significant in social settings. Different cultures and individuals have varying expectations of personal space. Violating this space can lead to discomfort and conflict. Thus, recognition and respect of personal boundaries is crucial for positive interaction.

Aside from space, our bodies manifest our discomfort or delight. Hence, it's crucial to watch for micro-expressions that can leak emotions even when people strive to conceal them. A quick grimace of displeasure, an eye roll of annoyance, or a smirk of satisfaction, these expressions, although fleeting, disclose much about the person's internal state.

9.3. Deciphering Nonverbal Signals in Educational Spaces

In an educational environment, nonverbal cues play a pivotal function in enhancing or impeding learning.

Teacher's body language significantly impacts the classroom climate. Positive nonverbal cues like smiling, nodding, and maintaining eye contact can create an engaging and reassuring learning environment. On the contrary, negative cues like frowning, lack of eye contact, or crossed arms can create a hostile or indifferent ambiance, hampering learning.

Students' nonverbal signals, like slumping in seats, avoiding eye contact, or excessive fidgeting, can express discomfort, disinterest, or lack of understanding. Teachers attuned to these signals can timely modify their teaching methods or address student's concerns.

9.4. The Interplay of Nonverbal Signals in Intimate Relationships

Nonverbal communication underlies the chemistry heard in the whispers of sweet nothings or in the silence between two individuals sharing a comfort zone.

Touch, a highly influential nonverbal cue, communicates a lot in intimate relationships. Depending on the context, a gentle touch can convey compassion, affection, or reassurance. Prolonged or unwanted touch can generate unease or indignation. Hence, understanding the 'touch code' and its underlying consent is significant in maintaining healthy relationships.

Gestures and postures also play a vital role. Subtle cues like mirroring each other's sitting positions, gestures, or coordinated walking patterns are strong indicators of connection and rapport in intimate relationships.

From boardroom battles to intimate encounters, and from social soirees to classrooms, nonverbal signals shape our interactions in unimaginable yet profound ways. Gaining fluency in this silent language equips us not only with the ability to convey our messages more effectively, but also with the power to decipher the untold stories that dwell in the silence of our wordless world. When you 'listen' with your eyes, you unlock an endless realm of deeper connections, nuanced understandings, and captivating interactions. Be a beholder of this world with enhanced and enriched eyes, learn to decode nonverbal signals. After all, silence speaks volumes when words fall short!

Chapter 10. Speak Fluent Body Language: Expressing Yourself Effectively

In the dance of life, your body leads, articulating your thoughts and emotions effortlessly, even before the words can escape your lips. The secret lies in nonverbal communication, the tacit dialect of gestures, expressions, and postures that can express torrents of emotions, meshing seamlessly within the melody of verbal communication. By understanding this language, you break free from verbal constraints and communicate more efficiently and effectively, leading to deeper connections and more potent interactions.

10.1. Understanding Body Language

At the heart of spoken dialogue lies the core elements of expression—our bodies. Often, the loudest speaker in a room is the silent one, making their point with folded arms, a firm stance, or firm eye contact. To unpack these silent messages, one must understand the vital components of body language:

Exercise patience and focus while observing as body language is subtle. Never isolate a gesture or posture; instead, consider it in the context of other physical movements and the situation at hand. Accompanied by verbal dialogue, a smile might radiate genuine joy, while in stern silence, it could indicate nervousness or discomfort. Remember, body language is a symphony, not an assortment of isolated notes.

10.2. Building Blocks of Body Language

Each element in our body contributes to the bigger picture of our nonverbal communication. Here, we break down these primary components:

- **Facial Expressions:** One of the richest sources of nonverbal communication are the features etched on your face: your eyes, lips, eyebrows, and even your forehead.

- **Body Posture:** The way you stand, sit, or move around contributes significantly to the message you're trying to convey.

- **Gestures:** Handshakes, nods, finger pointing, crossed arms – these are a few gestures that hold deep nonverbal meanings.

- **Eye Contact:** The eyes are often called 'windows to the soul' for a good reason. They can subtly yet powerfully convey your thoughts and feelings in an instance.

- **Proximity:** The physical distance between you and the person you're communicating with makes a difference.

- **Mirroring:** Mirroring someone's body language is often a signal of agreement or acceptance.

Remember that these components constantly interact, creating a chorus of nonverbal messages that boldly speak the language your words may not fully encapsulate.

10.3. Reading Expressions Right

Expressions are visual manifestations of our emotional state and thoughts. By honing the ability to read expressions, you seamlessly glide through conversations, empathizing better, and understanding others' mental states.

- **Smile:** Transcending cultural boundaries, a smile often represents happiness or amusement. But it may also mask anxiety or discomfort. Identify these subtleties by noting accompanying indicators: A genuine smile crinkles the eyes, while a nervous one might twitch at the corners.

- **Eyebrow raise:** A raised eyebrow often suggests surprise or disbelief, while the furrowing of brows implies confusion, concern, or anger.

- **Eye contact:** Direct eye gaze typically signifies interest or attentiveness, while avoiding eye contact can indicate discomfort or lack of interest. Remember that cultural norms heavily influence this aspect of body language.

- **Lip biting:** can signify nervousness, deep thought, or attempts to suppress an emotional response.

Remember to base your interpretations on the person's baseline behavior, situational context, and cultural background to avoid misunderstandings.

10.4. Mastering the Art of Nonverbal Communication

Now that you've unlocked the fundamental elements of body language, it's time to infuse these into your own self-expression. Be it a personal conversation or a professional setting, applying these principles can considerably alter the dynamism of your interactions.

- **Posture:** Stand tall and maintain an open posture to exhibit confidence. Avoid slumping or crossing your arms, which could be perceived as disinterest or defensiveness.

- **Eye Contact:** Maintain a comfortable level of eye contact to show engagement, but avoid staring, which could come off as aggression or make the other person uncomfortable.

- **Facial Expressions:** Make sure your facial expressions align with the message you're trying to convey. If you are happy, let your face show it—not just with a smile but with eyes sparkling with joy.

- **Gestures:** Use open-palmed gestures to signify honesty and transparency. Avoid aggressive motions such as pointing or closed fist actions.

- **Proximity:** Respect personal space. If someone steps away during a conversation, it's likely a sign they need more space.

In mastering these skills, don't forget to be mindful of the cultural nuances of body language. What might be standard in one culture could be disrespectful in another. Always approach other individuals with respect and a willingness to understand their unique cultural norms.

10.5. Conclusion

Embodying fluent body language does not happen overnight but starting to understand, interpret, and integrate it enhances your personal and professional life by broadening communication capabilities. When all else fails, seek clarity through direct verbal communication. And remember, body language is a conversation—listen as much as you speak, and your silent dialogues will become a rich tapestry of meaningful exchanges.

And with that, your journey towards becoming a master of nonverbal communication begins. Enjoy the dance—the symphony of silent communication awaits.

Chapter 11. Cultivating Sensitivity: How to Interpret Body Language Accurately

The capacity to accurately understand another person's body language, or nonverbal communication, is an essential and powerful tool in interpersonal communication. It enhances sensitivity to other's intentions, feelings, and motivations and allows us to respond accordingly.

11.1. Fundamental Elements of Body Language Interpretation

Nonverbal communication is a complex code that can only be completely decrypted by considering its various components in context. When trying to read and understand body language, sensitivity must be cultivated not only toward specific signals but also toward how these signals interact, align or conflict with each other:

1. Facial Expressions: These can be incredibly subtle, yet, when interpreted correctly, they can provide valuable insights into a person's feelings and emotions. Key facial expressions to watch for include those conveying happiness, sadness, disgust, surprise, fear, and anger.

2. Body Postures: The way a person stands, sits, or moves can reveal much about their attitudes and intentions. For example, a slouched posture can suggest disinterest, fatigue, or sadness, while a rigid posture may reveal tension or anxiety.

3. Gestures: These can range from emphatic hand movements and head nods to subtle, possibly even unnoticeable, thumb twiddling

or foot tapping. Each gesture carries specific meanings and can provide insight into a person's mental and emotional state.

4. Distance: The physical space maintained between individuals during interactions, also known as proxemics, can indicate their relationship and comfort levels.

5. Eye Contact: This aspect can demonstrate the level of interest, trust, or dominance during an interaction.

6. Touch: This can communicate support, emphasize a point, or establish dominance. It can vary significantly in different cultures and settings.

Remember, each nonverbal cue must be read in relation to other cues, within the context, and should align with the spoken words for accurate understanding.

11.2. Facial Expressions: A Window into Emotions

Facial expressions are perhaps the most obvious and immediate form of nonverbal communication. Our capacity to recognize and interpret these expressions is innate; however, honing this ability requires careful observation. A warm, genuine smile may signal friendliness, pleasure, or approval, while a tense and thin-lipped smile might betray anxiety, disapproval, or insincerity.

Limited eye-contact, or a rapid shift in gaze, may suggest discomfort or avoidance, while steady eye-contact can demonstrate interest or assertiveness. Raised eyebrows indicate surprise or disbelief, and a furrowed brow is often a sign of confusion or concern.

Understanding these variations in facial expressions can be pivotal in discerning the subtle undertones of communication.

11.3. Discerning Meanings Behind Postures

A person's posture provides valuable clues about their attitudes, level of engagement, and emotional state. Open postures, where arms and legs are not crossed, suggest openness to interaction and a relaxed state of mind. On the other hand, closed postures, characterized by crossed arms or legs, often signal defensiveness or withdrawal.

Changes in posture can also provide insights. For instance, an initial open posture shifting to a closed one may indicate discomfort or diminishing interest.

11.4. Interpreting Gestures

Gestures often accompany our words to provide additional emphasis or clarity. Rapid hand gestures can communicate excitement or urgency, while still hands might suggest calmness or control.

Closed fists can signal anger or frustration, an open palm is often seen as a sign of truthfulness or submission, and pointed fingers can express accusation or emphasis.

11.5. Proxemics: The Language of Space

Physical space can speak volumes. Close proximity might signal comfort, familiarity, or assertness. In contrast, increased distance can indicate feelings of antagonism, discomfort, or submissiveness.

Recognizing these spatial codes is critical when interacting within different cultural contexts, where personal space norms may differ.

11.6. Seeing Through the Eyes

Prolonged and fixed eye contact can signal attentiveness, interest, or challenge, while constantly avoiding eye contact can be a sign of deception, discomfort, or disinterest.

However, like the other elements of body language, eye contact should also be interpreted in context. For instance, in some cultures eye contact can be seen as disrespectful or confrontational.

11.7. The Power of Touch

Touch serves as a critical nonverbal cue and contributes significantly to the overall quality of an interaction. A firm handshake can express confidence and sincerity, a pat on the back can show support or affirmation, while an unwelcome touch might signal intrusion or dominance.

Understanding these body language components will equip you with a refined sensitivity towards the subtleties of nonverbal communication, enabling you to interpret body language confidently and accurately. Complement this knowledge with empathy and respect for cultural differences to become proficient in reading body language.

Remember, communication is not just about speaking and listening. It's also about observing and interpreting. Cultivating sensitivity towards body language lets you perceive what isn't said, tells you when words don't align with actions, and allows you to respond fittingly.

This sensitivity empowers relationships, enables effective communication, fosters understanding, and provides an edge in negotiations. It is the key to unlocking the vast and vibrant world of unspoken communication, enriching your interpersonal experiences, and fostering healthier, more meaningful human connections.